Boredom

How to Eliminate the Feeling of Boredom

(How Doing Nothing Can Boost Creativity and Productivity)

James Barnett

Published By **Regina Loviusher**

James Barnett

All Rights Reserved

Boredom: How to Eliminate the Feeling of Boredom (How Doing Nothing Can Boost Creativity and Productivity)

ISBN 978-0-9950956-3-2

No part of this guidebook shall be reproduced in any form without permission in writing from the publisher except in the case of brief quotations embodied in critical articles or reviews.

Legal & Disclaimer

The information contained in this book is not designed to replace or take the place of any form of medicine or professional medical advice. The information in this book has been provided for educational & entertainment purposes only.

The information contained in this book has been compiled from sources deemed reliable, and it is accurate to the best of the Author's knowledge; however, the Author cannot guarantee its accuracy and validity and cannot be held liable for any errors or omissions. Changes are periodically made to this book. You must consult your doctor or get professional medical advice before using any of the suggested remedies, techniques, or information in this book.

Upon using the information contained in this book, you agree to hold harmless the Author from and against any damages, costs, and expenses, including any legal fees potentially resulting from the application of any of the information provided by this guide. This disclaimer applies to any damages or injury caused by the use and application, whether directly or indirectly, of any advice or information presented, whether for breach of contract, tort, negligence, personal injury, criminal intent, or under any other cause of action.

You agree to accept all risks of using the information presented inside this book. You need to consult a professional medical practitioner in order to ensure you are both able and healthy enough to participate in this program.

Table Of Contents

Chapter 1: Boredom Phenomena............. 1

Chapter 2: Is It Because We Are Bored?. 15

Chapter 3: What Makes Someone So Bored? 47

Chapter 4: How To Prevent Burn Our... 105

Chapter 5: The Causes Of Boredom 144

Chapter 6: Strategies For Managing Boredom In Individuals With Adhd 159

Chapter 7: The Role Of Medication 168

Chapter 8: Supporting Individuals With Adhd 178

Chapter 1: Boredom Phenomena

The research on boredom has shown that boredom is an important influence on various aspects in a person's daily life. The feeling of boredom is universal. Most people suffer from it at some point in their life. Current estimates from surveys show that between 30 to 90% of American adult suffer from bored at least once throughout their lives and 91 percent to 98 % of teenagers. Males are more likely to be unhappy more than females.

While the feeling of being bored is commonplace, the sensation of boredom goes back in the human past. The subject has been of fascination since the early Greeks. Based on Susan Matt, a history professor at Weber State University and one of the co-authors of Bored, Lonely,

Angry, Stupid The root of this concept dates way back into Ancient Greece. "So it was that the early Greeks were using the term 'acedia that referred to lack of concentration which was a reference to lack of energy. The early Christians utilized it in relation to monks that went in the desert and lived in solitude, and were overwhelmed by a feeling of sadness that caused them to lose their faith in God," Matt says.

While there are indications to suggest that early Greek philosophers thought about boredom as a concept however, it took time before a term that referred to boredom was introduced. The word "boredom" was not introduced into the English vocabulary until 1766. There simply wasn't a need for such an expression. Thus, (excessive) boredom seems to be a fairly novel phenomenon. Furthermore is the amount of individuals suffering from boredom has risen due to the advancement of technology. But, the study of boredom goes back around 1885 at the time that British scientist Francis Galton published a short note in Nature entitled 'The Measures of Fidget', his report of the way in which his audience participants behaved at the course of a conference.

However, over the years there were very few people expressing a genuine concern for the topic. "There are many things around us that we aren't able about, perhaps due to the fact that they seem trivial," states John Eastwood, a psychologist who works at York University in Toronto, Canada. The phenomenon started to alter in the year 1986 when Norman Sundberg and Richard Farmer from the University of Oregon in Eugene created their Boredom Proneness Scale (BPS) which was the first method for researchers to gauge boredom, which went aside from asking the participants "Do you find yourself overwhelmed?". Instead, they would determine how many people agreed or disagreed with a statement such as "Time never seems to stop" going by too quickly", "I feel that I'm performing below my ability majority of times", "I am not able to keep up with my work most of time" as well as "I enjoy being able to keep myself entertained".

The field is growing. In May The University of Warsaw drew almost 50 people to their second annual boredom conference that attracted speakers from around the world from sociology and social psychology. Then, in November Danckert brought together around twelve researchers from Canada as well as from the United States for a workshop in the field. Researchers across fields that range that span from philosophy to genetics, the humanities and psychology are beginning to collaborate on boredom research, claims John Eastwood, a psychologist in York University in Toronto, Canada. "A large number of individuals working on similar problems creates movement."

Most people experience boredness at time up to time. Different age groups could be more prone to boredom than other. The majority of adolescents experience boredom. Although they have more options to decide what they want they do in their time however, they're immersed in learning about themselves as well as their passions. Inexperience in deciding where to concentrate could cause boredom.

When it comes to studies on binge eating, such as boredom, is among the top factors frequent triggers of anxiety and depression. A study on distractibility with a driving simulator the people who are more susceptible to boredom were driving at a higher rate that other participants. They also were slower to react to dangerous situations and drove more often across the middle distance. In a study conducted in 2003, US teenagers who said that they are often bored were 50percent more likely than less bored peers to eventually become addicted to drinking, smoking and other illegal substances.

Boredom is even responsible for around 25% of the variance in the student's performance, according to Jennifer Vogel-Walcott. She is the developmental psychologist from the Cognitive Performance Group, a consulting company based out of Orlando, Florida. It's the same proportion that is attributable to natural intelligence. The word "boredom" is "something which requires a lot of thought" according to her.

The definition of boredom is an arduous task. Researchers have characterized boredom in terms of various outcomes that are that are associated with boredom. These include the level of arousal, focus, understanding of a situation and cognitive. According to some research, "It seems to be the kind of mental state individuals find uncomfortable, a absence of stimulation which leaves people wanting relief and has numerous behavioral, medical and social effects." Cynthia D. Fisher, psychologist, describes it to be "an uncomfortable, temporary affective condition in which an individual experiences a general lack of attention and has trouble focusing in the present activity."

"In the traditional sense boredom refers to often a psychological and emotional condition that occurs when a person has nothing specifically to do, or isn't at all interested in their surroundings or believes that a particular time or day is boring or monotonous." The most commonly utilized description of boredom can be described as "the unpleasant experience of longing for but not being able to do something enjoyable".

Boredom's feeling is commonplace and is a regular part of every day life across a wide range of societies. It is a normal feeling. Being unhappy with an activity and not interested to it, may cause feelings of boredom. The signs of boredom can be in situations where you are feeling energetic, but aren't able to focus your energies. This can also happen when you are unable to focus upon a particular project. It is a frequent complaint in adolescents and children. The feeling of boredom is common. Finding yourself unsatisfied with a task or not interested to it, may cause feelings of boredom. The signs of boredom can be when you feel enthusiastic however you are unable to channel your energies. This may happen if you are unable to focus to a particular task.

Are you feeling bored? Are you unsure of what you can do with your time? You can't find something that is interesting? If yes, then you may want to get involved in something but it's not intriguing or enjoyable. We all know this grumpy condition. Everyone has been through it. It's like being trapped in between doing something, but not being able to come up with something that you want to accomplish. This isn't because it's not your intention to engage in things. But, every task that you think of is dull and dull.

The term "boredom" refers to not being able to identify meaning and is an extremely discomforting experience. The feeling of being bored can result in a sense of emptiness. Feeling bored may cause you to feel drained, or disengaged. It can be a problem particularly if you're trying to finish a significant assignment for work or school. The stress can trigger other issues like anxiety, depression, fatigue or loss of interest or interest even laziness and other non-task connected and frequent results.

The feeling of boredom can be a indication that you're doing something which doesn't bring you joy. It could indicate two things: you're not completely present and absorbed in the current activity or the task you are working on isn't meaningful for you.

It is common for people to feel that your work is unimportant and uninteresting. If you believe that you're being forced to complete tasks that do not serve any purpose or aren't pursuing an objective that is meaningful then you're likely to feel negative about your work.

It is the result of the ability to pay attention. A person who is bored may not be energized. Feeling unfulfilled, you may be aren't able to sense an emotional connection with your surroundings. The signs of boredom may manifest as two different things: fatigue (feeling exhausted) or anger (feeling annoyed).

It isn't as easy as you imagine it to be It is a multifaceted issue. While you may think of boredom as an easy experience, studies have revealed that there exist two kinds of boredom.

Indifference is feeling bored of everything in the world. The feeling of indifferent boredom is when there's no reason to be concerned. There's no interest in the world within you. You could be thinking about something else, staring at the sky, or feeling as if you're going to fall to sleep. This is how you may experience during an especially boring course in math.

Feeling stuck and powerless to improve the circumstance. Being bored and apathetic is the result of boredom, which is often triggered by feeling of insecurity. Apathy can be a sign of feeling of boredom when you feel stuck within your circumstances and are unable to alter your situation. The boredom that you experience is common among teenagers and may be an indication of depression.

The Boredom Proneness Scale (BPS) has opened possibilities for research that were previously unexplored and revealed that boredom referred to anxiety as well as and the quest for meaning, as well as the feeling of ennui. It's served as an launching pad for many various boredom scales, and as a trigger to make the field more prominent and an instrument for linking boredom and

A few studies have revealed that there is a link between the desire for sensation or risky behaviour and high boredom-proneness ratings. Results from research released in Science in 2014 as well as Appetite for 2015 contain research reports. In the initial study, researchers asked individuals to be in a quiet room without anything doing for as much as fifteen minutes for an time. A few of them, specifically men, were prepared to receive tiny electric shocks instead of being left to think about their thoughts. In the second report, researchers included two studies where the participants were able to enjoy endless sweets and that gave them the option of endless electrical shocks. The participants ate more food in times of boredom -and they also received additional shocks. While it may not be particularly pleasant it is more exciting than monotony.

Chapter 2: Is It Because We Are Bored?

Symptoms & Causes of Boredom

According To Fromm boredness is "perhaps one of the main causes of violence and destruction in the present." The people who scored low on the boredom-arousal scale were observed to perform better across a variety of areas of their lives such as education, career and independence.

The sign of boredom is the feeling of being empty and feelings of anger over this feeling of emptiness. If you're bored and you're not sure why, you might be unable to pay attention and have a low attention to what's happening in the world around you. It's possible to feel depressed and fatigued. You may also feel anxious, anxious or even jittery.

Being unhappy with a particular thing, or feeling uninterested by the subject, could cause feeling bored. The signs of boredom can be when you feel energized however you are unable to channel your energies. This can also happen in the event that you find it difficult to focus on your task. Uncertainty about where you should focus may cause frustration.

There are many reasons to being bored and it isn't a rare occurrence. People are unhappy or anxious for different reasons, leading them to become increasingly bored. The reason for this is that it feels like you're under no control when you're in a hurry or rely on others to complete the job done. It happens when you are not in the ability to control your circumstances. The problem with boredom is in the event that it prevents you from accomplishing the tasks you require or reduces the quality of living.

Every person is afflicted with boredom once the course of time. The inner processes that result in feeling boredom are well-known to researchers. The main cause of boredom is (among many other factors) lower concentrations of the neurotransmitter known as dopamine. Dopamine can be described as a chemical transmitter that is found in our brains. It stimulates our brains when we are exposed to an exciting and new situation.

Repeated repetition of an task, however, lowers how much dopamine is released to the brain. In turn, the amount of dopamine that is released in the brain decreases. This means that we begin to crave an increased sense of joy and are unable to provide the same with our current tasks. This is the point at which the sense of boredom begins to manifest. It's no longer exciting to engage in familiar activities and have to work for new and interesting alternative ideas. This is in line with the thinking of, John Eastwood and his colleagues define boredom as feeling desire for something however, not being able take part in a task satisfying the desire.

It is common to experience boredom in situations in which there are lots of sources of distraction, which threaten to take our time to fill it with items that do not really appeal to us. The world is flooded with information through websites, YouTube as well as streaming platforms. With this in mind, one might believe that boredness isn't a thing anymore but it actually exists, though more subtle ways. No matter how many stimulations that we are exposed to - the heart problem is the extent to which we're unaware of how we utilize our time whether it's or not. time or not.

The study of 1989 revealed that a person's perception of boredom could be affected by their degree of concentration, because an increase in the acoustic levels of distracting from the surroundings was associated with greater reports of boredom.

"Banishment Room"/a "banishment room"A "banishment room" or "chasing-out-roomA "banishment room"/ a "chasing-out-room" "boredom space" is an effective approach to managing employee departures that involves employees being transferred to an area that assigns them meaningless jobs until they feel demoralized enough to leave.

Recent studies have revealed that boredom-related proneness is evidently and frequently associated with lack of concentration. Yet, some individuals occasionally find themselves in a state of boredom. But, many people are susceptible to this. Though boredom is typically thought of as an insignificant and minor irritation, the tendency to boredom is associated with a wide variety of psychological or physical, academic, and other social issues. The signs of boredom are when you are unable to pay concentration. It could be due to the fact that your mind is overwhelmed by the many factors in your environment. If you're feeling stressed over something else or your current situation can be too stressful, you could find yourself feeling overwhelmed. The reason for this is that you are unable to think about anything else other than the thing that's making you feel stressed.

The occurrence of boredom-related proneness is believed to be linked with a lack of and attentional slips. The absence of interest is an indication of boredom which many are experiencing in everyday life. If they are suffering from an absence of mind the sufferers show symptoms of memory loss and low recall of recent incidents. The absence of mind can cause a variety of impacts on daily living It can also be a longer-term, more serious issues.

Blaise Pascal's Pensees examines human nature in writing that "we are seeking rest during an effort to overcome obstacles. Once we've conquered the obstacles, we find that rest is unaffordable due to the boredom it creates",

In the absence of any stimulus or focus one is confronted by insignificance, meaninglessness of life, and suffers from an existential fear. Heidegger says by saying: "Profound boredom, drifting through the depths of our lives as a fog that muffs takes all objects as well as oneself in a stunning absence of. It is a sign of being all-encompassing."

Erich Fromm and other thinkers of critical theory talk about boredom as an essentially reaction to the industrial world in which people are forced to perform work that is not their own. According to Fromm and others, the quest for excitement and newness that is the hallmark of consumerism are not the solution to boredom but are merely escapes from boredom, which is, as he says, carried on in a state of numbness. In addition to aesthetics and personality The most common cause of boredom can be found in the waiting process, like Heidegger observed, for instance at the front of a line, waiting in anticipation of someone else's arrival or complete their task or when one travels in a different location. Cars need quick reactions which makes its owner active and, possibly because of other motives it can make the trip less enjoyable despite it being completed earlier.

The term "boredom" can refer to a type of learnt helplessness that is a condition closely connected to depression. A few parenting theories assert that children should be placed in a space that is devoid of stimulation, and they aren't allowed or instilled to be involved with their surroundings in a meaningful way, they won't develop the cognitive capacity to be able to do this.

If someone tells you they're bored, what should you suggest to them? You suggest they look for an exciting new pastime? Go to a different place? Do something that is useful? Most likely, you wouldn't suggest that patients speak to their physician concerning depression. If you're feeling depressed disinterested, bored and depressed motivation is a sign of depression. This is especially true when it lasts for longer time.

Boredom is a sign of boredom in a variety of ways, however here are some common instances:

There is a lack of interest in the initiatives

It is difficult to remain interested longer than short periods

Not able to relax or rest.

There is no feeling of excitement

The difficulty of staying focused

Boredom is experienced by people in a variety of ways. in different ways. Boredom can be caused by:

Insufficient sleep or food

Low levels of stimulation for the mind

Lack of control or choice on your daily routine

Insufficient variety of recreational activities

A poor understanding of time

The boredom you experience could be due to depression, if you have these symptoms:

feeling hopeless

Feeling sad

Avoiding stimulation opportunities

You are blaming yourself to bore you

Impact of Boredom

The researchers believe that prolonged boredom can lead to health concerns which could then decrease the duration of your life. As with stress, boredom can create unnecessary pressure and increase the risk of heart attacks. It is possible that boredom can be a result of bad lifestyle choices that can lead to heart disease:

smoking

alcohol misuse

substance use

Mindless eating, binge eating or feasting

Consuming unhealthy food

What causes people to be bored? The feeling of boredom can trigger transformation and provides the opportunity to reflect. Thus, this feeling could occur during work that's not demanding or highly repetitive. The reason for this could be the lack of awareness about what makes us happy. Personality characteristics also have an impact on the way we feel. Those who are more inclined to sensation seeking or extraversion are more likely to feel bored.

The cause of boredom is when your energy doesn't get channeled to the direction that brings fulfillment or purpose. However, this is a mix of a few important elements. The first is mental arousal. being energized enough to spend on something exciting. The second issue is having difficulty staying focused on one task. Another is the an inability to control the surroundings around you, like at a wait room or in a lecture room, when it is impossible to shift your focus to something else.

An investigation in 1989 suggested that an individual's perception of boredom could be affected by the degree to which an individual pays focus, with a greater frequency of the acoustic signal being distracted from the surrounding environment is associated with more frequent reports of boredom.

Lethargy

It could be a natural reaction to boredom, insufficient sleep or overexertion and stress, insufficient exercising, or it could be a sign of a condition. As normal responses, the feeling of lethargy usually resolves after enough rest, sleep and less stress and a healthy diet.

Perception.

A person's surroundings are dull monotonous, boring, and deficient in excitement. It could be due to the lack of leisure or artistic interests. When in a classroom the most common reason for frustration is the lack of comprehension For instance, when you aren't following or comprehending the content during a lecture or class the material will appear boring. But the reverse can be the case in that something which is readily understood, easy to understand or clear, could seem boring. The opposite of boredom can be associated with learning. Likewise, in the school setting, it can indicate that a child is not sufficiently challenged, or is not engaged. Any activity that seems routine for students is more likely to cause boredom.

Environment:

A person's surroundings are dull monotonous, boring, and deficient of stimulation. It can be due to a lack of inactivity and lack of artistic interests.

It is a sign of depression that is clinical. It can also be a manifestation of learnt helplessness that is often closely connected to depression. Certain parenting theories suggest that if kids live in a world that is devoid of stimulation, and not permitted or taught to be involved in the environment around them, they'll not develop the capacity for mental stimulation. engage in this way.

Incomprehension:

In the context of learning one of the main causes of boredness is the ignorance in particular, when you aren't following or engaging with the subject matter during a lecture or class and it appears boring. The reverse could happen when something is easy to comprehend, straightforward or clear, could become boring. It is common for boredom to be directly connected to learning. And at school, it could be an indication that a child is not sufficiently challenged, or is not engaged. Any activity that is routine for students is more likely to cause them to be bored. There are many reasons to being bored and it isn't a rare occurrence. Indeed, those feeling bored could be unhappy or anxious for different motives, which can cause them to be increasingly bored. The reason for this is that it feels like you're under no choice if you're waiting on some thing or you have to depend on another person to accomplish the job done. The feeling of boredom is in situations where you don't have the control over your circumstances.

The problem with boredom is in the event that it prevents people from doing the things they need to do or reduces your quality of living. If you suffer from anxiety, you could be more susceptible to depression following lengthy times of boredom.

Monotony in the Mind

The term "boredom" is akin to fatigue, and it is due to repetition and a disinterest when it comes to the specifics of our work (such for tasks that demand continual attention, like waiting in the airport, or prisoners inside cells). Anything that's predictable and routine becomes monotonous. It is generally true that repetitive repetitions of the same things and not enough stimulation could cause the victims an absence of interest and an apprehension of being trapped.

Lack of Flow

Flow refers to a state of absolute immersion in an activity that's challenging but with one's capabilities similar to "being at ease." Flow happens when the skills of a person are in line with the challenge that is presented by the surroundings and when the task has specific goals as well as immediate feedback. The tasks that are easy tend to be dull. On the other hand, jobs that are perceived as too demanding can create anxiety.

A need to have NoveltySome people tend to be more bored than other people. Individuals who have a constant need to be entertained, exciting and variety have a higher risk of being bored. People who are awe-inspiring (e.g. skydivers) will likely find that the world is at a slow pace. Needing stimulation from outside might be the reason extroverts seem to be the most susceptible to boredness. The pursuit of novelty and taking risks is a way individuals self-medicate their boredness.

Paying Attention

It is a sign of problems in concentration. We are not able to gets our full interest. It is difficult to get engaged in something if you are unable to focus on the subject. The people who suffer from chronic attention disorders including attention-deficit/hyperactivity disorder, show a significant rate of boredom.

Emotional Awareness

Self-awareness is a factor that makes people more likely to be bored. The person who is bored can't to express the things the person wants or would like to accomplish. They are unable to articulate their emotions. Inability to determine the things that make people satisfied can cause deeper boredom in the present.

Uncertain of what we're seeking means we are unable to determine the most appropriate goal in our interactions with others.

Inner Amusement Skills

People who lack the capacity to handle boredom in a constructive manner depend on stimulation from outside. If they lack an inner source of entertainment external stimuli is never able to provide sufficient excitement and variety.

Lack of Autonomy

A lot of people experience boredom whenever they feel trapped. Being trapped can be an important aspect of being bored. In other words, they're restricted or trapped so they are unable to be carried out. As an example, adolescence can be an era of boredom at its highest mostly because kids as well as teenagers do not have much control over their choices.

The Role of Culture

In various ways, boredom has become a luxury of the present. The concept of boredom was virtually nonexistent prior to the 18th century's end. It was created when the Enlightenment began to give its way into the Industrial Revolution. The beginning of human history was in the past, our ancestors were forced to make the biggest expenditures

Insufficiency of energy

The main reason for fatigue is a lack of energy or imbalanced levels. It could, for example occur where you're physically exhausted however physically any point exhausted. This is because boredom can arise when your body is physically active while you're exhausted by your mental capacity and the reverse is true. A great solution for such boredom is to get involved with an activity that utilizes the energy that is abundant. A graphic designer with a lack of mental or creative energy might choose to engage in a physical exercise. However a worker in construction could attempt to take part in (creative) tasks that demand the highest concentration levels.

Procrastination

A lot of times, individuals think they're bored when in the actuality, they're merely procrastinating. There's a big distinction between feeling bored and doing what you can to delay obligations. If you're bored the situation, you're unable to come up with a worthwhile task to take part in. If you're in the second scenario the problem is you're putting off dealing with things aren't your favorite. This is why boredom could arise from the inability of one to come up with something else you could delay your work on. This kind of uneasy state can be eliminated quickly by figuring out what responsibilities/tasks you're postponing and why.

Lack of motivation/inspiration

Most of the time, boredom is caused by a lack of proper motivation or the right inspiration. If this is the case there is no reason to be bored because of lack of an activity that is interesting to engage in. In reality, we're just discontent because we do not have an appropriate motivational factor to engage with a particular thing. Nearly all things will seem dull and monotonous. It's vital that we are constantly reviving our enthusiasm and motivation. Inspiring yourself can help in getting over boredom.

Pattern interruption

A different cause for boredness could be due to the abrupt interruption of your routine. Meaning that your schedule has suddenly/unexpectedly changed. As a result, this unplanned pattern change is typically the sense of becoming extremely exhausted. The best solution to combat the feeling of being bored is to continuously seek out interesting and exciting things that can quickly fill your timetable. There's also alternative of using your increased freedom to individual growth through contemplation and reflection.

Want to be a part of something

In the time of technology most of us are familiar with being bombarded by details. In addition, many of us are reliant to this kind of entertainment. In the absence of it, people are uncomfortable. We've gotten so used to being always doing things, even if it's simply watching television, that the idea of not being able to complete something is a bit odd. Being idle feels like a burden and makes us feel resentful and at risk. In the end, the idea of living closely ties with what we do to the majority of us. Thus, being idle can be the final punishment for crime. If we look at it in a more granular way into its simplest form, boredom is simply a need to entertain yourself or do some thing. This is simply the brain's need to have (more) stimulation.

The combination of restlessness and boredom is a bundle

Restlessness and boredom are part of an entire package. If you're uneasy, insecure, says Osho. Find out the cause of restlessness and boredom. If you're feeling bored, you'll want to get away from that particular situation. When someone is talking to you that you're annoyed, you will begin to anxious. It's a clear sign that you're looking to move off from the place, and away from him, the petty talk. The body begins to move. Naturally, due to respect for others, you avoid it. But the body itself is moving since the body is more real than the mind. The body is more genuine and genuine than the mind. Your mind tries to appear courteous, and looking at you with a smile. The mind says, "How beautiful," however, inside your head you're thinking, "How horrible! I've listened to the story numerous times, and now he's repeating it!"

"Whenever you are bored, you'll feel restless. The feeling of being restless is indicative of your body. The body says, "Move away from here. You can go anywhere, but you shouldn't remain there." However, the mind keeps smiling and your eyes keep glowing, and you carry in saying you're attentive and never had the pleasure of hearing something so beautiful. Minds are civilized but yet the body is wild. The mind is human, but the body remains an the animal. The mind is a lie; the body is real. The mind understands the laws and rulesthe way to conduct itself and behave in a manner that is right and, therefore, when you encounter a boring person, it is possible to say "I am incredibly happy that I am so pleased to see your face!" And, deep inside, if permitted, you'd kill this person. The man entices you to commit murder. You become agitated, the next thing you know, you are feeling restless. If you pay attention to your body, and then run away, the anxiety goes away. Do this. If someone seems boring to you, can simply jump and run around. See. The absence of restlessness just indicates that the energy is not wanting to stay in this place. The energy is already in the move. The energy has left the place. Then, you are following the energy." Therefore, the main thing to do is understand the concept of boredom and not a sense of restlessness.

Are you able to recall?

It is evident that the intellectuals, those who have too much to think about can be more irritable, because they are thinking. In addition, due to their thought processes, they realize it is simply repetition. It is your life that repeats. Each day you wake up in the exact same manner as you've been doing throughout your entire existence. Your breakfast is taken similar to how you eat breakfast. You then go to work in your office -- it's exactly the same place, same staff, and the same working. You return homeand the same wife. If you are bored, that's normal. It's difficult to discern anything new here. Everything is old and covered in dust.

Bertrand Russell is reported to say, "When I remember, I can't recall any more than a handful of moments that I truly was alive and in awe." Do you have any memories? In what moments of your life where you were truly burning? Very rarely does it happen. People dream about these moments and imagines the times, and one longs for those times But, it's not the case. However, if they happen eventually they become monotonous.

Become more conscious

If you are in an affair with a woman or even a guy and you experience a moment of bliss however, by the end of the day it's gone and all is the routine. routine. It is the feeling of repetitiveness.

Thus, individuals try to make a change. When they move to a brand new home, buy the car they bought, they get divorced from their previous husband or find another love interest and then that process will become routine eventually or at some point. Changes in location, people and partners, or changing homes, aren't going to make any difference. If a group is bored, the people are forced to relocate from one city to the next, From one place of work to the next or from one spouse to the next. But sooner or later, they realise that it's all just a flimsy idea since it's going continue to occur for every woman, all men, at every home, and with each car.

How can I help? Become more conscious. This isn't a matter of changing circumstances; change your own being and becoming more mindful. When you are more aware, you'll be able to realize that every second is a new one; however, for this, a huge amount of awareness is required.

Chapter 3: What Makes Someone So Bored?

Symptoms & Causes of Boredom

Feeling bored may make you feel drained and not motivated. It can make things worse in the event that you've finished some important work at or at home. Focus on the final goal in completing your job or task. The benefits.

"Is existence not just a million times too brief for us to be bored?"- Friedrich Nietzsche

In 2014, for example researchers under the direction of psychologist Reinhard Peckrun from the University of Munich in Germany revealed that they followed 424 students from the university over the course of the academic year. They measured their levels of boredom as well as recording the scores they scored on their tests. The researchers found the evidence of a pattern in that boredom correlated with lower exam performance and this led to more students being disengaged from the class, and also higher level of boredom. The effects of boredom were constant all through the year when you take into account the students' gender, age and motivation to learn or intrinsic motivation as well as previous accomplishments.

The signs of boredom are feelings of loneliness, anger ("cabin fever") and sadness and fear. Like Kierkegaard said that boredom was "the source of every bad." If you are continuously bored, you have a higher chance of developing drinking addiction, drug abuse, as well as compulsive gambling. In the long run, boredom can raise the risk of developing an early-onset cardiovascular disease. Boredom is a reason that it can cause stress hormones to increase in your body. Boredom can also be linked to an entanglement to depression. In certain cases, continual boredom can trigger depression. But you might have a chronic boredom from being afflicted with this mental illness.

Strategies to Overcome Boredom

"I'm bored" is an unhelpful way to express your feelings. It's true that you're in a vast, huge and vast universe that hasn't seen a single inch of. The inner world of your mind is infinite; it goes through the night, within are you aware? Being alive is wonderful, which means it's not possible to claim that you're bored."-- Louis C.K.

Are you feeling bored? Do you not know how to spend your time? Are you unable to come up with anything exciting to do? In that case, you could want to get involved in something but it's not intriguing or enjoyable. Everybody has experienced this frustrating situation. Everyone has been through it. The feeling of being bored is that you are stuck in between doing something, but not able to come up with something that you want to accomplish. The problem isn't that you aren't interested in doing things. The problem is that everything that you think of is dull and monotonous. So let's make it more interesting! There's no need to be frightened because of boredness. There's an entire, vast universe out there waiting to explore it. Find out how to fight boredom. Allow it to motivate you and make use of it to battle boredom.

It is commonplace for people of every age, but some boredness is inevitable. But, learning to handle boredom from an early age can develop the ability to solve problems that will be helpful in the years to come.

It is possible to combat boredom with three different strategies. It is crucial to know what boredom means and why it's causing. In addition, it is essential to come up with strategies you could implement as soon as boredom starts to set in. The third measure to fight boredom consists of having a set of activities that will can help you break free from boredom.

Enjoy boredom and do not fight it.

In today's ever-busier environment "not working" is believed as the most sinful thing you can do. Therefore, many people suffer with boredom, and the sense of not being productive that goes from the feeling of being unproductive. Contrary to what many believe there is no reason at all essential to stay constantly doing something. In fact, it's not required to enjoy technology all time.

Therefore, instead of being in the face of boredom Try to take advantage of these moments. Take pleasure in having nothing to do to think about. Take advantage of the fact that you don't need to accomplish. Take advantage of your time to relax and recharge your batteries. In the end, you'll find that boredom begins to go away.

Discover the direction you want to take your life

An absence of orientation. It is possible to be afflicted due to not knowing what direction your life is heading in. If this is the case your boredom can be a result of wandering around life with no having a clear goal and goal. It's as you're just not confident about the direction that your life will take.

Unable to find your inner compass in order could make you feel isolated and in a state of paralysis. Then it's time to get rid of that! Your life can be steered to the right way through a thorough examination of the goals and your goals as well as your purpose and goals throughout your the present. Finding the most appropriate course for your life consists in large part of reflection and evaluation of your strengths as well as weaknesses. In addition it helps to better understand what you could be doing with your existence.

Be surrounded by energetic people

It is possible to become addicted to boredom. Think about the most recent time you spent your time with a very boring, dull, and uncreative individual.

It's just the matter of time until you got bored also. Being constantly around those who engage in monotonous and dull actions will eventually draw them into their world and vice versa. But in interacting with fascinating people, you'll find some new and thrilling things.

Socialize

It could also be an indication that you are in need of a fresh source of input. Social input it will help you stay on track. There's a myriad of ways to beat boredom that you could perform on your own, however at some point or another, we will do all appreciate the company of other individuals. Human beings are social creatures which is why it's natural that boredom may arise as we become isolated. If this sort of boredom begins to set into our lives, social interaction is the most effective method of getting over the issue. Meet strangers. Make contact with your friends and spend time together. Even if they are working it is possible to take part in a club that interests you or get involved in charitable activities.

Find out something completely new

Get rid of boredom by identifying ways to stimulate your mind. It is common for boredom to manifest when we reach an optimum level of proficiency at a given task. When this happens, you may feel bored. This comes from being unchallenged. Therefore, instead of becoming comfortable with your accomplishments constantly strive to discover something completely new. Try to push yourself with unfamiliar activities that you've never attempted previously. Explore the world of unknown. Find a new skill, or learn a new language. Learn a new language or read a book on something you've never seen previously. In whatever you do, be sure to learn about something you've never heard of before:

Go through a Wikipedia or other. article each day

Visit the local library to pick up one of the interesting books

Explore different intelligent YouTube channels

Visit an institution you've never been to previously

Explore Reddit (for instance"Today I Learned")

Ask your family and family members to teach you the most important skills.

Discover the environment around you

Visit an exhibit

View a documentary

Reduce procrastination

Doing things that you don't want to do can create boredness. The problem is when you're not in a position to locate a motivating distracting activity to keep your attention away from your work. However it is important to do all you can to put off the task. But, on the other hand you'll find nothing to distract your mind from you. In the end, people simply drift off to dream or indulges in non-essential things. One way to handle this issue is to tackle your responsibilities which will not only stop the procrastination habit and putting off work, but be able to eliminate boredom too.

Clear your 'to do' list

A state of boredom provides a fantastic occasion to cross off the things you have on your "to complete to do' to-do list. There are a lot of tasks you've always wanted to complete and never got the ideal time. Now is the ideal time to do it. If you can't come up with anything else and you are driven to finish the task, the things accomplished is quite strong during periods of intense bored.

Do not over-think.

If someone is confronted by boredness, two main things take place. They first feel awful. They then start to overthink. They think endlessly about the issue. They are bored, and immediately seek a solution. In the end, they look over the problem, but they cannot escape themselves.

Sometimes it's best to stop thinking too much. You shouldn't ask yourself all sorts of concerns. Do not try trying to figure out how you can get over your boredom. This will only make the situation more difficult. This will just make you feel a little more ill. If you're feeling bored. Let it be. It's a phase that is temporary. It's not necessarily bad in and of itself.

Change up your routine

It's a key reason for boredom. "Men have only routines." It's quite easy to continue following your routine repeatedly. But, habits and routine are also important reasons for boredom. When you repeat the same routines repeatedly eventually, boredom will gradually begin to appear. To combat this, you should try to break up your routines every now and then. Incorporate new ideas and look for ways to approach things in a different way. You can try a few not to do the same routines. It will give you more freedom.

This can help reduce boredom, monotony and the resulting boredom. There are plenty suggestions to spice things up in your daily routine:

More often travel.

Explore the new surroundings.

Get out and meet people you have never met before.

Try different things.

Alter the time you perform things.

You can change the way you approach problems.

Do not waste your time with a mindless pursuit

Let yourself be overwhelmed

When boredom begins to surface, we swiftly attempt to eliminate it through a variety of activities. There are those who watch the TV for hours while other people briskly surf the Internet. However, the feeling of doing nothing productive or being extremely frustrated remains. It's because we'ren't willing ourselves to feel feeling of boredom. The goal is to let it go from it instead of facing the issue openly.

There are times when you should take a moment to let yourself be at times, you should allow yourself to feel bored. When you let yourself feel uninterested every time to time it will help you get closer to the root of the issue. Start digging into it. Then you'll be able to identify the main motives behind it. In certain instances it could be that you're procrastinating. There are times when you're not having motivation. In other instances problems, the issue is more deeply. Perhaps you're trying to shield yourself from trouble by cutting off from the outside world.

Be in the flow

The term "boredom" could mean an opposite to the state of flow. We do not focus to a particular activity instead, it is centered on the misery you feel when you are we are bored. Discover enjoyable activities that enable people to return to their flowing state. Anything that allows you to completely immerse yourself into the activity, which takes you away from your normal your self, time and space. Explore the tasks that enable you to get into the flow. The activities include gardening and drawing, to cooking, writing solving problems, inventing and other sporting activities.

Start writing

If you're feeling exhausted, you may also use this time to reflect and write. It's not even difficult. Simply grab a piece paper, or even open an document and begin writing down anything that comes to the mind. Reminisce about what has occurred to you throughout the course of your day. Think about the possible solutions to the issues that you're facing. Journal about your goals as well as your plans to realize these goals. There is no wrong or right when it comes to writing. Do it as you please and observe what happens.

Beware of mindless pursuits

How many of us haven't sat and watched television, not being entertained? It's likely that we each spend a bit of time browsing the Internet for no reason. What's wrong of these activities that are mindless can be that they provide nothing of worth. In the end, there is a good chance that they will make us more bored. If you're faced with the opportunity to choose, ensure that you select an activity that will bring real benefit to you since boredom can result from an inability to focus on meaningful activities.

You must challenge yourself If you're always confronted with boredom, then there's a chance you're missing out on things that really test you. They are those that satisfy your requirements and needs rather than just reaping those low-hanging fruits.

Make something using your hands

The joy in making things. If you keep your hands active and creating, you not only lessen boredom but change your mind away towards the technological aspects of your living. It doesn't take much to be a master craftsman or an expert artist. All you need is the intent of turning the idea into a the real world. It is possible to draw a beautiful image, crochet a scarf, or make a work of work. What ever comes to thoughts is good.

Quiet reflection & meditation

The majority of people looking at effective ways to fight boredom are in desperate search of interesting and new ways to get involved. However, introducing new sensations will only be effective over a limited amount of time. Once the time is over, people soon become bored. In this way, fighting boredom could be a complete vicious cycle. It's because none innovative activities are able to deal with the root cause of boredom.

Meditation is a way to address the core issue with any type of boredom. It's far more efficient than constantly looking ways to get involved in. It's because meditation rapidly enhances your ability to be at ease with not doing. Meditation is a powerful instrument to combat boredom. Meditation can help you raise your tolerance level to not being occupied or engaged. Furthermore, studies have demonstrated that mindfulness is an exercise in meditative can help reduce boredom.

The ability to master

There is a chance to be lucky enough to win the lottery and get millionaire overnight, but there is no way to master their trade through random chance. If we're discussing artists, athletes or academics The story is identical. If you are looking to reach your potential, you need to be practicing a certain ability for a prolonged time and with a remarkable level of consistency. Develop new abilities as well as crafts.

The focus should be on the result of the work, rather than the work itself.

Focus your attention away from your task in hand to focus on a final result. It could be an outcome of the behavior you're striving to achieve. In other instances the result is something you come up with. As an example, you could create a game around staying active even when you're not enjoying the exercise the exercise.

Explore and Identify

One of the best ways to combat boredom is to investigate the reasons you are bored at all in the first place. If you find the activity you're enjoying isn't beneficial for you, maybe it's time to think about ways you can engage in better opportunities in the future. If you're in a circumstance that you aren't able to manage, meditation may make you feel less bored quickly. If you're faced with an uninteresting work project doing it quick may be the ideal alternative.

Are Exiting objects a thing?

Utilize dull time to be productive. Do something that you've put off for a while or master a new technique. Gather with friends in times of boredom and search for interesting things to do in your town. Find ways to be entertaining. Even if you're at a loss for ideas, just because you're not enjoying the house doesn't mean that you cannot take a break and enjoy a bit of laughter.

Relax and have a laugh.

Physical Activities

If you're feeling bored taking advantage of your time through getting some exercise to help. Being active in your body will assist in keeping your mind busy. This can ease bored. You don't have to do a strenuous activity. It's as easy as taking a stroll. Take a stroll along the street, through in the downtown area, or even to the park. If you're an artist type, carry a sketchbook or camera for capturing interesting experiences. Swim. If you are a fan of sports choose your favorite one such as basketball football, soccer, or tennis. In case it's raining take a break and do some stretching in the indoors. You can do this inside and keeps your body in shape and fit.

Do yoga. It is a great way to build the strength of your body. Yoga can also ease the boredom. Yoga is an approach to life that revolves in embracing and being present to the moment. Becoming more conscious of your own and the world around you can help lessen anxiety. There are many Yoga routines that are guided on the web. Take the time to learn and practice.

Discover a new technique.

This is ideal if feel bored frequently. Making time for an exciting new pastime or activity can give you the assurance of many productive hours in the future. If you're not artistic take a look at learning how draw, paint or craft. Many tutorials are available on the internet. If you're not musically talented take a look at learning to play or sing. If you're bored or have a difficult time, practice the instrument in your the comfort of your home. If you like cooking, you can purchase a book to cook something new every single day. Make a meal from a food which is totally new to you, like French as well as Thai.

Plant your garden

The act of gardening and creating a garden is beneficial for both the physical as well as emotional health of your family. Go to an area greenhouse and purchase various seeds and plants. Learn more about the best ways to take care of the seeds you purchase. If you don't have a garden Many homeowners keep vegetables and fruit plants on their balconies. There are also small potted plants inside

Plan your next trip or events.

If you're not looking for anything to do, it's a good idea be smart to plan in advance. If you're overwhelmed, make plans for any you can think of for your next trip or event. If you did not have a firm idea of the Christmas schedule yet check out the flights you have booked and check your schedule. It is also possible to make smaller ideas. Like, perhaps you and your buddies are talking about going bowling. Set up a Facebook event to invite everyone to attend.

Organise your house.

If you're bored there's every day something in your home needing attention. Perhaps your shelves aren't properly alphabetized. Perhaps you've got a ton of clothes that you're not yet hung within your wardrobe. If you're feeling bored, try some organizing in your house. It will provide you with satisfaction and will also help to reduce the frustration. If you are looking for inspiration about how best to organize look up some websites for interesting ideas to make your house less cluttered.

Take action on something you've put off.

Everybody puts off some chores. Perhaps it's time to finish those tasks. It will keep you busy while you get something that you've been dreading and get it done with. Perhaps you don't like doing laundry and yet you've heaps of it piling up. If you're tired it's a good idea to complete the laundry.

You can play an online game with your buddies.

A few games, including Checkers, chess or Monopoly need additional players. If you do not have any players playing, phone applications and gaming consoles let you to play online with players on the internet. Also, you can browse the internet and locate games you can enjoy. A lot of people enjoy playing card games on the web, like. Play a few cards games. There are some that can be played alone like Solitaire. Other games, like Uno and Slap Jack, require more players. Utilize your phone. Perhaps all of your friends have played an online Trivia Game via your smartphone. Look around to see if there are any people who are interested in playing this moment. Contact friends on the game console. A lot of video game consoles let players to participate in games alongside other gamers.

Try some basic, no-prop games when you have friends who are around. If you're hosting guests playing games, you can play them. Certain games only require your voice and a some imagination. There are games you can play such as I-Spy and Truth-or-Dare. You can also play Twenty Questions Trivia Game etc. Connect with friends on the game console. Some video game consoles permit gamers to engage in interactive games alongside other gamers. You can try telling a story with your friends. Each person should add a sentence to the tale. It can be either verbal or written. You can play improvisational games, such as the charades. Find patterns in clouds (or rocks for those who live in an area that is mountainous and rocky). It's a fun game that stimulates the imagination. Play a few card games. Certain games can be played by one person like Solitaire. Other games, like Uno and Slap Jack, require more players.

Go to a cafe shop.

If you're lonely and uninspired and there's no one is around to help go to the coffee shop. Find out if a good friend you have in mind would like to meet for a coffee. Invite. Talk to your pal with a cup of coffee. A good chat is a wonderful way to alleviate boredness. If you don't have anyone for a chat, head the local cafe by yourself. It's possible that you'll meet someone sitting by themselves and might be able to strike up an exchange. It can help ease the boredom of your life and also help create a new friendship. It is possible to leave a message in the shop. Examples include, "Wow, I really am in love with the ambience of this shop."

Go back to old films with other friends.

If you're spending time with other people in the same age, you might want to look up older films. The process of re-watching your childhood and teenage favorites is a fantastic method to relive some nostalgia and also reduce boredom. If you don't have anyone who you can watch classic films with, consider whether a person you know would like to see the exact same film that you're enjoying and talk over it by text messages. It can be like being invited to a party.

Take a look at cute or funny images on the internet.

Internet is the perfect way to amuse your self. You can search for something like "Cute pug images" and then spend time time taking in adorable photos of dogs. Also, you can look through videos of adorable animals or cute baby animals to help pass the time. If you're talking with someone else who's frustrated, the two of you can send video clips or pictures you come across of adorable things on the internet.

Visit an antique store.

There's no need for a ton of money for shopping. If you're bored but financially strapped, pop at your local thrift store. There are a wide range of brand new clothes at a reasonable cost. If you don't in buying something but it's fun to try out the funny clothes you discover at an auction store.

Take a trip as a tourist around your city or town.

In the event that you and your buddies have no idea what to do, just pretend that you've never visited your city prior to. Set aside a time to visit every local attraction and dining at the local establishments. It's a great opportunity for you and your group to go back to places in the town that you might consider as a luxury. Are those visitors often there? Visit a local museum, or hike on the nature trails in the area. Do you have a favorite restaurant you can try to grab a bite?

Do a photo shoot.

Use smartphones or cameras to capture pictures of you with your family and friends with a range of postures. There's even the option of going outside to take pictures of your outdoor adventures. There's no need to take an intense photo shoot even if you're not feeling at your best. It's okay to take humorous photos to make you laugh later.

Take a look at an ebook.

It is an excellent technique to let your mind forget you're bored. The words of an author could help you enjoy an escape from your mind. Books for young adults and children excel at this. They also can bring out the child in you and evoke emotions of nostalgia and wonder. Choose a genre you enjoy. If you've not been able to explore sci-fi, the science fiction genre is likely to cause the boredom. Choose instead to read traditional fiction. If you do not have available books, take a trip to the local bookstore or library. Going out could help reduce boredom.

Draw, paint or draw Something

It's a fantastic method to use your imagination. Also, you'll have something stunning to display after you've finished. Additionally, it can assist you to learn a new skill which is a great thing to practice when bored. Drawing or drawing may boost your mind's IQ. Doodling is believed to aid in staying engaged and focused by stimulating your brain. If you enjoy painting and draw but you're not exactly what you should sketch, you can try taking a walk outside by drawing a still of the things you observe. It is also possible to create or paint interesting things within your home. It is also possible to sketch or paint your favorite film or book character If you're looking to exercise your imagination.

Colour

Coloring can be a fantastic method to reduce boredom. Find the crayons and markers, as well as a coloring book. Coloring for just a couple of hours will help you get bored.

Write a list

Lists can be a fun way to get through the time. Make a list of destinations you'd like go to, books you would like to read and goals you wish to accomplish. It is also possible to create an unintentional list with no important goal. You can create a list that will force the reader to consider various suggestions. As an example, you could list 50 songs for Christmas or 50 girl's names beginning with the "A. "A." It is also possible to make lists of the things you love. You could, for instance, keep a list of your favorite movies of specific genres as well as your most cherished books and your most favored places to travel.

Create some writing that is creative.

It doesn't require you to be an expert writer to be able to accomplish this. The act of writing a few words may be challenging for you personally and will help to ease frustration. Writing helps you to divert your thoughts. It will help you focus on the task you're doing, instead of thinking about how boring you are. If you're having trouble starting write, you can just start a blank writing. Record anything you think of without filtering your thoughts. If you find something intriguing, you can try to develop that idea more. It is possible to begin with writing something such as "I'm completely bored" and then describing what you are bored of. If you're a fan of creative writing begin writing your novel, poem or short story you've thought of finding the time to create. Make with a blog. If you find it a bit odd to blog without a specific goal in mind, you can start writing about something that you're interested in. As an example, you could begin blogging about music in case you are a fan of going to shows.

Send an email or letter.

If you're feeling bored and want to think of someone who whom you'venn't been to in the past few years. Consider writing them an email or letter. This will help you accomplish some good work by contacting the person you want to reach out to and also reduce the frustration.

Offer something encouraging to your family member. As well as reducing boredness, you'll have a better feeling in your self. Say to someone that you're thankful they were able to help you in a particular like that or you were impressed by the way they dealt with a problem. You might want to write a letter for soldiers overseas and disaster victims as well as someone who is in an assisted living facility. There are numerous organizations that take letters from the public and mail them to the recipient. If you sign up to this kind of group, you'll always find something you can do even if you're bored.

Create gifts for your relatives or friends.

If a holiday is nearing, or you're feeling generous, give a gift. There's no need to be an expert crafter to create gifts that are cute and meaningful to someone special to you. Make something as simple as making a flowerpot out of clay and making a photo collage with the construction paper and stickers for a hand-made card. If you are a knitter or crochet, you can try creating the perfect scarf or arm warmers. These are simple to complete in just a few hours. Make a scrapbook with your loved ones. Find a scrapbooking album or a blank notebook with some pictures, paper as well as glue and ornaments. It is possible to create pages on a particular theme. In this case, for example, on a page, you might include images or mementos of a certain holiday.

Utilize household items to make craft projects.

If you're feeling bored and trapped at home There are plenty of activities you can create using objects that are lying around your home. These can alleviate your boredom, without having to shell out more money or travel. Make a fun night light by filling up a mason jar full of old Christmas lights. Additionally, you can stick the lights on the sides of the mason-jar into an elegant style. Are you a homeowner with sewing equipment or older pillows? You can sew several pillows to create a longer body cushion. If you're a parent with young children it can be a great idea for sleepovers. Do you have lots of keys in your house? Get some nail polish on and paint the ends of every key in a different shade. It will be easy to find the key you want when you need it.

Avoiding Boredom

1. It is important to be aware that intense arousal levels can lead to a feeling of boredom. It is possible to

associate boredom with an uninteresting environment or being exhausted and sleepy, but it is also possible to be uninterested when overloaded by external stimuli or are very energetic in their own body and can't focus due to this. You might be feeling bored in a noisy cafe, with high-pitched music, and lots of chattering people. The reason for this could be a result of the external stimuli of the sound suffocating the person in front of you, or distracting your attention from working. You might even believe that you're bored due to the fact that you're sputtering with energy and can't remain focused on just one thing for longer than a second or two. Energy levels can rise from everyday sources, for example, being well rested or having anxiety over an upcoming flight. If you are experiencing this stimulation, you may mistake this as the feeling of boredom.

If you're feeling overwhelmed by the outside world, take steps to decrease the intensity. In case, for example, the environment you are in is loud and you are unable to sleep, wear headphones and listen to music or white sound. Also, consider going somewhere that has less interruptions. If you're extremely energetic You can try something that will help to burn off some of the energy you have, like walking. Return to what you did after your walking.

2. Stay off the computer, internet and couch. If there's a program you're dying to see Avoid using television or other media for filling your time. The result is that you think about things you'd prefer to be doing. Research has shown that

this could increase the intensity of boredom.

3. Avoid daydreaming. Thinking about different places or things that you would like to do will only increase boredness, not ease it. Being caught in the midst of a daydream can make you feel like your activity is dull, even though you normally consider the activity stimulating. If you like to indulge in a time-consuming task, such as cleaning the floor or mow the lawn can be a great chance to get into a daydream. The tasks that require only a only a little "presence" will not be significantly altered by your dreaming.

4. Make a list of the activities you will be doing each daily activities. If you see any big gaps in your daily schedule attempt to fill them in by doing things that interest you. It is possible that you are dissatisfied and bored at daily at the

same time. It's an excellent idea to make a plan to include an activity that you can do for these hours to help avoid the feeling of boredom.

5. Get involved in social activities. Join an organization or youth group to enjoy a planned time or plan out a date for yourself with your buddies. If you're bored and feel like there's no time to entertain yourself and you're bored, there's a better option to beat boredness than to be with others. Get together with your friends to plan some sort of outing or invite the neighbors to join in some basketball games in a group. Even if it's just going to the mall together and having coffee, you're trying something different. Get together with your old group of friends or reconnect with former acquaintances to change up your routine. Face-to-face networking. Don't use social media websites in lieu of

socializing, and get to know individuals in the flesh. Attend events. What's happening? Spring Break? Christmas Break? Summer? Check out fun camps you can make plans to attend during time off. time

6. Pause to prevent tasks from becoming boring. Recent research has shown people who took two-minute breaks throughout an uninteresting 50 minutes of work were more relaxed, focused and more productive when they finished the work. If you're embarking for a lengthy project Give yourself something you can be looking forward to by queueing for an YouTube video, track or article you're eager to read and then reward yourself for 30 minutes of productive work by taking an unintentional 2 minute break.

Take a break from your desk to take a few minutes. If you only go to the kitchen for an iced drink the few minutes you spend there could be refreshing. Take a stroll through your garden and enjoy the flowers for breath of fresh air.

7. Quiet your workspace. There is a popular belief that turning off the TV or radio playing silently in the background can provide a tranquil and productive work environment. It's true that this can divert your attention to an unconscious scale. The result is that you are more miserable than if worked in complete silence. The ability to concentrate on a single task regardless of whether the task can be described as "boring," is a better idea than splitting your brain into competing stimulation. Make use of radio or music to get rewarded instead of a distraction. Stopping for a few minutes over the course of an boring exercise will ultimately make your work more efficient instead of trying to complete

the task with no breaks, and letting radio conversations play as background noise throughout.

8. Control your blood sugar. If your blood sugar levels decrease and you begin to notice you're finding it harder to focus on your job. Have healthy food items like fruits or nuts at the office to help keep your brain to its maximum capacity. You can reward yourself with a little bit of chocolate when you've completed the most difficult homework task or set of memos from the workplace. Energy drinks as well as other sources of caffeine are a hit and are a good choice, however, the "crash" that is associated with these drinks can affect your performance for the longer term. Beware of these stimulants in order to prevent from getting back into boring rut.

9. Keep active. There are people who prefer to work on exercises balls instead of chairs or various other office furniture that allows you for staying active. However, it doesn't require an enormous amount of cash to move. Going out for a short walk or taking a few minutes to perform a simple stretching routine in the bathroom can boost your energy levels and help keep your concentration to stay focused. If you're running you can work on the treadmill desk. The act of standing and working from a standing position is proven to be an effective and healthy way to keep your focus.

10. Find a job or join a become a volunteer. If you find yourself having too much free time look into some part-time work or even volunteer. Earning money or helping others can fill your spare time with a purpose that will leave you happy. Here are some tips to help you get

started: Retail establishments like stores, as well as cafes are fantastic locations to find an occasional job. They typically provide flexible hours of work which makes them perfect for those who are students. Nurseries, hospitals soup kitchens, hospitals, and shelters for animals are usually in search of volunteers. Apart from being enjoyable and satisfying, volunteer tasks like this appear attractive on resumes or application forms.

Consider being self-employed. It's possible to help take care of lawn maintenance for people as well as walk their dogs or even babysit. If you're crafty and creative, you could even create items, like bags or scarfs which you sell on the internet.

12. The term "boredom" refers to not being able to identify meaning that is an

painful sensation. Instead of trying to get rid of it, plunge yourself into it, so you will be able to discover what could provide satisfaction to get over the feeling. Eastern civilizations have always recognized the importance of accepting boredom and believe it is an avenue to greater consciousness.

A great way to get rid of boredom could be to look into your reasons for feeling bored initially. If you find that something isn't worth your time for you, maybe it is time to think about ways you can engage in better opportunities in the near future.

13. If you are in a circumstance that you cannot control, meditation may make you feel less bored quickly. In the event of the monotony of your work doing it fast may be the most effective alternative. Consider the task as a kind of

meditation such as "bus-waiting meditation" transform it into a chance to practice breathing exercise. Make sure to take time to think about the aspects of your life that you're thankful. Think of it as a researcher or journalist looking into what exactly you are experiencing boredom. These techniques and more can change the way you view your experience.

14. Regulating Cognitive Demands

Be sure to focus on projects that you manage mentally. Don't overwhelm your brain with too much stimulation.

15. Adjusting Cognitive Resources

Find out which stressors you are dealing with and how well your brain can be for tackling different projects. Be sure you're confident enough to manage the task and not overload yourself.

16. Managing Goal Values

Journaling can be a great means of determining your objectives and the tasks that are most important to you. The process will enable you to concentrate on things that matter to you, keep your mind and help you stay engaged.

17. Switching Activities

It's the most effective method to overcome boredom since it raises your interest and allows you to focus on new tasks. After you've identified the primary of your boredom's cause You can find other ways that you could try to keep active. This includes:

18. Finding the perfect new activity

Involving yourself in a community

Are you thinking about a change in career direction?

Exercising

More time with family and friends

19. Support and Resources

It can cause you to feel depressed, exhausted and hopeless. It can also make you feel uninterested, depressed or irritable and a host of other unpleasant emotions. It is difficult to make changes in your life because boredom is reducing your motivation and focus. If your boredom has a negative impact on your overall quality of living, it might be time to find help. Think about contacting a therapist or a psychologist who can assist you in overcoming boredom, and discover the motivation and drive to live your daily life.

55 amazing activities

to instantly end boredom

1. Imagine your day as you were an operative

2. Check out TED talk

3. Get out and enjoy nature

4. Be awestruck by your stars (stargazing)

5. Take a nap

6. You can listen to audiobooks

7. See people performing all kinds of ridiculous activities

8. Invent exciting stories

9. Explore the city in your free time

10. Take a trip around the globe

11. Participate in conversation with strangers

12. Write poetry

13. Learn to speak a different language

14. Learn a strategy game

15. Enjoy a relaxing bubble bath

16. Explore a museum of contemporary art

17. You can be a mentor for anyone

18. Picnic at the park

19. Do a good deed

20. Do volunteer work

21. Visit a Renaissance fair

22. Design a vision board that reflects your dreams and goals

23. Create and sing your own tune

24. Start a book/movie club

25. You can cook something you've never cooked previously

26. Go to an art exhibit

27. Find a solution to a crossword puzzle

28. Write a note to yourself in the future

29. Allow your mind to wander thinking about your daydreams

30. Begin painting with numbers

31. Change the layout of your Facebook profile

32. Send surprise postcards to your friends

33. Collect images from old magazines

34. or newspaper

35. Enjoy the sunrise and sunset

36. Write a bucket list

37. You can host a themed night of movies

38. Complete a puzzle that is challenging

39. Study the art of calligraphy

40. Play charade games

41. Start a family scrapbook

42. Record a playlist or CD with the music that has influenced your life

43. Board games to play

44. Do some research on a topic

45. Make sure to take pictures

46. Design your own YouTube video

47. Make a drawing

48. Create your own short tale

49. Go to standup comedy shows

50. Take time playing with pets

51. Go through a book

52. Take a class in yoga

53. Enjoy a classic film

54. Create your personal tongue

55. Costume night? Make the music louder

And imagine that you're playing in a live performance

Chapter 4: How To Prevent Burn Our

Signs of Burn Out

Do you feel like browsing through Instagram due to the fact that you're exhausted to read a book? Are you buried in debt? Or do you do you feel as if you are working constantly? time and feel the it's time to do whatever brings you happiness and transform into a profitable business? Are you feeling like you have an interminable to-do checklist? In the midst of several years of organizing, controlling your goals, and exceeding them as well as tackling obstacles, you realise that you do not take a lot of interest in the work you do. Activities that used to be exciting like inspiring, leading and innovating don't mean any more. It's time to stop burning out.

The term "mental burnout" was coined in the 1970s as a way to explain the psychological consequences of constant working stress, can occur in such a subtle way that one could quickly mistake the signs as other negative influences that can cause stress, such as a cold or an unfavorable boss. Since cases of burnout have increased at an alarming rate throughout the years In 2019 the WHO declared burnout as a medical condition that is a major health issue which can lead to "increased anxiety about one's work" as well as "reduced effectiveness as a professional." according to the definition, the term "burnout" refers to the term used to describe a condition that arises from stress at work which hasn't been effectively controlled.

It is a condition of total physical, mental and emotional fatigue. It is caused by anxiety, stress or stress that is excessive that is often associated with feeling stuck and stymied, as well as being in a state of only a little control. Sigmund Freud remarked many years ago that we feel just the sense of utter helplessness. In 1989, Austrian author Peter Handke, in his "Essay about Tiredness" says "Thus we sat enjoying our exhaustedness. A cloud of exhaustion that was ethereal, was what held us all together." Rahaf Harfoush, a Canadian worker expert and writer of the book "Hustle & Float', says that, even without an actual workplace it is possible to experience burnout when at home and is more likely in the present due to the increased pressure of the coronavirus pandemic.

Take a look at the physical and psychological symptoms that are that are associated with stress: Depression, anxiety sleeplessness, impaired immunity as well as loss of appetite, alcohol abuse and depleted reserves of energy. These all suggest a loss in control and taking full control of the situation. The idea that burning out is simply a matter of choice or excessive activity can be a means of reassuring us that we're not in a position of powerlessness and that we are the kings of our homes.

The person who is burned out is exhausted but is cannot find the time to the time to rest. This is the main difference between burning out from just plain fatigue. When a person is exhausted and is able to feel that the work finished, their fatigued muscles and drained capacity for energy may bring an immense satisfaction and prepare the body for restorative sleep.

"The most prominent symptoms can differ but usually starts with something like an increase in anger, feelings of overwhelm or overwhelmed, inadequate sleep or a feeling of fear when you go to work or school (if it is the primary cause of stress) frequently followed by nausea and the feeling of being stuck or entrapped in a circumstance. What to observe in people around you or a significant change in behavior, they could develop a tendency to be shy, avoiding or negative. Their productivity may decrease."

These symptoms may resemble depression, and if left untreated could become extremely serious and even crippling. It is true that there are less severe symptoms and everyone are susceptible to experiencing varying degrees of emotional and mental anxiety, particularly when confronted by the uncertainty. Becoming aware of yourself and recognizing the indicators is essential so we can be able to take care of our self and make time for self-care."

Do I Have Burn Out

Signs of Burn Out

1. You are on all hours of the day, and you've got very little or even time to devote yourself to self-care regardless of how it appears for you. It is clear that you are not able to distinguish between your home and work. There's a possibility that you're at work all time which is affecting your health to the point which you're feeling exhausted in the extreme. There's no time to cook, or due to your fatigue and grumpy, you're making unhealthy selections.

2. Procrastinate more now than ever before: You discovered yourself in the middle of working hard after you realized the advantages having a home office

completely free from distracting factors. The pace never dropped to an even and steady rate. In the end, you were procrastinating. It was an extremely productive week the previous month, and now feel that you're not equipped with enough brainpower or the bandwidth to do anything in the month. You've exhausted yourself.

3. It's like you're left with nobody to whom to turn in the event of a crisis Maybe you've had the experience of "too many people" within the office space previously. Thus it is important to keep your time and space for yourself is extremely valuable. However, working alone can be both a blessing as well as a negative. Connections that last are essential to both our professional lives as well as our private life.

If you're at work when a situation arises such as a problem with your computer, an entire team around you who can you turn for assistance. In the event that you're all alone with only the walls of your living space but you could be completely alone when trying to figure how to resolve the issue. You could even get yourself burned out doing so.

4. There is a constant fear to be more successful The tendency is be awed by others. "When I worked in the office I simply believed it was more efficient to leave only when someone else had left before me. If I was first to leave then I could not help but be concerned about how other people perceived my character." It's normal to think that people have more work and are longer than I am, therefore you should be working longer and more hard isn't it? Being longer-working doesn't always

result in better performance or in reverse. It's just a matter of burning yourself out.

5. It's a habit to check your email notification every day I'm addicted to my email. I keep checking my inbox using my mobile more frequently. If you also are constantly checking your workplace communication apps at every hour of the evening and day, it's likely that you're burning yourself out.

6. It's letting meetings run over their designated time blocks. When you are working from your home, you're likely to have make phone calls or take part in video-based meetings each and every so often so that you can stay in contact to your colleagues and managers. It's crucial to inform everyone of what's happening at work and make sure everyone on the team can be on the

same page. Without a commitment to rules and boundaries, you may exhaust yourself.

7. It's time to stop "adulting" completely
The consequences are a significant strain on your brain when you begin to become unmotivated, which can happen. It is a good idea to exercise and sit for 30 minutes of meditation each day before diving directly into the work.

8. Finding it difficult to motivate yourself
Burnout is a common symptom that decreases interest in daily activities and hobbies. An absence of enthusiasm among IT individuals about new technologies is an obvious warning signal. "When terms like "blockchain" and 'IoT' trigger an exasperated sigh and shoulders that slump You're witnessing burning out.

9. If you're feeling tired and there's no way to ensure that sleep or rest is enough to provide replenishment then it's time to look at the reasons behind it and consider why. After medical causes are ruled out The most likely reason is stress. "IT is a 24-hour huge, expensive and high stakes sport and it's exhausting."

10. IT executives are often expected to provide rapid, exact solutions to difficult problems. However, numerous IT problems, like glitches in the hardware or problems with cloud services, are only resolved by external service providers. This usually requires time. The constant distraction of these issues may cause concentration issues.

11. A short-tempered personality: Engaging in arguments with colleagues as well as family and friends as well as

suddenly feeling feelings of general frustration or anger that is consuming could be a warning sign of something going not right. It can lead to resentment and can manifest both at work and the home. "Individuals who are suffering from burnout have to deal tension, both at the workplace and in their homes," Under chronic stress working that at first enjoyable and exciting may become a burden and cause sadness, according to Jacinta J. Jimenez, psychologist at Stanford University.

12. Health problems: More frequently stomach troubles, colds and other ailments that you are accustomed to may be an indication of exhaustion. "Along with the psychological effects of putting the body into an uncontrollable stress level could have an impact on the immune system, and it is possible that

you will come up with illnesses more frequently as opposed to the norm."

13. All the time thinking about work There's no need to constantly be thinking about work-related issues during holidays or weekends But when work-related thoughts are constant and insistent burning out is a real chance. Most professionals do not have the capacity to switch off their thoughts when they're working. However, this behavior could be detrimental and stress-inducing. The list of things to do never seems to shrink, which causes anxiety and could lead to depression. It's hard to perform because everything seems to be a top importance.

14. People suffering from burnout tend to develop "escape behaviors." "These can include consuming unhealthy alcohol, or drinking and other behaviors

that attempt to avoid." Remember that burning out doesn't occur suddenly. "It isn't an "on/off" thing.," Burnout is really more subtle and slowly destroying healthy habits as well as other individual traits, like shaving or bathing. "Your body and brain are sure to warn you however, you must pay attention ... to spot these early."

15. Relaxation Issues: Being unable to relax when you are in WFH can be a sign of burnout that is being under-worked. It's like you're always having to remain "on," and perpetually in a high level of alertness. There's a continuous stream of emergencies. Some of the most prominent signs of working too much are being unable to relax and feeling that there's too little time throughout the day to complete everything accomplished. The signs include not being able keep track of your tasks and noticing our

health decline by being overweight or losing weight. The line that separates your working and your personal life has become unclear.

16. Are you feeling that there aren't enough hours during the day: A lot of tasks require you to do tasks that require several people usually because of reductions in size. If coworkers get dismissed however, their work needs to be completed, this is then transferred to remaining workers. One sure indication that that you're on the job all the time is when you work overtime and is a routine element of your work. It's impossible to complete every task in a normal eight-hour work day. You are obliged to stay for longer hours at the office, or take the work back to home.

17. The list of things to do keeps growing The efforts you make to improve your

organisation are useful, but do not make the task completely achievable. The day begins with seven tasks that you must complete However, by the end of your day, the list grows to twelve things. When you finish your day, you may complete five items you needed to complete and your list gets longer.

18. Are you feeling like you'll never catch up Regardless of how quickly or effectively you do your do your job, you'll be struggling to manage the continual stream of assignments. There is a rare feeling of being finished in any task or undertaking or project, whether at the end each day week or month. You begin to fear gatherings, whether because they're so frequently scheduled or they are doing nothing more than cut down the time that you can use for productive tasks.

19. The health of your family is declining
It can occur through a variety of methods and in a variety of combinations. You're losing weight. It's so stressful that you're not eating. The weight gain is due to aren't finding the time exercising or eating. It is common for you to experience various ailments and discomforts with an unidentified root. The doctor has reported dangerous rises in blood pressure. You're on multiple medication including prescriptions and non-prescriptions in order to make it through your day. It's exhausting even which you're not working. You're interested in everything: families, friends, leisure and activities are almost zero, since you aren't "up for it..

Are you overly cynical? Have you noticed that your sarcasm is higher than it previously were? It's tough going and it's making you more critical.

20. Are you ready to go on a run Are you tempted to throw your entire life away and reserving an all-inclusive trip to Bali? Are you thinking about getting away from the world in the long run and moving to a home in the Caribbean? It could represent a sign of "worn-out burnout" According to experts. The avoidance strategy is another way to cope which is used to remove yourself from work or evade it due to doing too much initially believing that it can help you achieve more success.

21. There's an issue with your normal tasks: If you're having difficulties time making notes or focusing your thoughts engaged with daily tasks. Are you guilty of a myriad of mistakes recently? From forgetting to celebrate your anniversary, to rushing out of your breakfast An abrupt lack of concern for details could be a sign of burnout.

22. The fact that you're always tired and exhausted: exhaustion can be a indication that you're suffering from workplace inefficiency. Are you one to sleep in a dreamy sun-filled Saturday morning? The constant sluggishness could be an indicator to look for, especially if you discover that one or two days or two of "sleeping in" does not eliminate the feeling of fatigue.

23. There's Always A Little Discontent: You have a hard time keeping your cool working. You're adamant that your bosses have a bad reputation and that your coworkers are rude? The perceptions you make about your workplace may be the truth. However, these perceptions could cause "burnout. Then you could start to blame the culture of your workplace (for without a reason) for the self-imposed speedy rate "to reach the highest point."

24. If you're doubting your own abilities: find yourself wondering if what you're doing has merit? That distorted sensation of "reduced achievement" is an etiological sign of burnout that can be felt by any person who's had a hard time working.

25. It's a constant ache Have headaches that don't be gone? An upset stomach that is gurgling all the time? Are you suffering from a persistent breathing issue that bothers you? If your doctor isn't able to find any cause, think about a deeper look at your calendar of work according to scientists who have identified a variety of connections between the physical and mental health of employees and their burnout. Some times, work-related stress could lead to bodily harm. "Higher levels of burnout" according to one study's authors, "led to a faster pace of decline in the physical

condition," which ranges from colds to arthritis to heart issues.

26. Insomnia: Continuously pushing your limits in your work when you've exhausted your energy will harm your overall health. Stress from work can lead to fatigue due to sleepiness. Many people sleep in a comfortable home environment, however, they feel their exhaustion when they step in the workplace. These are both signs that indicate there is a problem with fatigue. Chronic fatigue can result in small mistakes, a lack of concentration and mood swings.

27. Trouble concentrating: Feeling detached from work can be a signal that you're overwhelmed. Particularly if you're trying to sort through multiple ideas at the same time and you're in a

state of disorientation and are unable to focus on your work you're working on.

28. Unbalance Food drinks, food, or smoking cigarettes can indicate that your brain is trying to escape into the activities that will allow you time to unwind.

29. Refraining from social situations: cutting your self off from social groups and relatives is an indication of stress, anxiety and sometimes depression. It can cause you to feel more lonely and can lead to an endless cycle.

30. Being Unsatisfied: Feeling that you're not good enough in your job is a sign you're experiencing burning out. Impostor syndrome is common to some extent however it could be very detrimental after an aforementioned point. When you reach the level where you believe that you're unable to

perform your duties and that you do not fit the job It can be difficult to improve your mood.

31. A Short Fuse: If you're experiencing unusual outbursts of anger or crying in the office and having constant arguments between your family and friends it is possible that you are being afflicted by burning out.

32. Physical ill-health: If you discover that you've taken time off from work because of illness such as flu or colds, headaches nausea, dizziness and headaches it could be because from stress. Stress can cause serious harm to our bodies.

Burn out - What Should I Do?"Burnout is a standard problem for the millennial generation which is marked by an increase in hopelessness and anxiety, which is exacerbated due to the pressures of having to "perform" our lives on the internet. "The Covid-19 epidemic has put people to long periods of increased anxiety. Recent research has revealed the fact that 40% of employees find themselves exhausted because of issues like remote work and working more hours managing family obligations, threatening employment security, and anxiety of workplaces that are unsafe. They have also led to long-lasting feeling of anxiety and sadness and a loss of motivation and lack of concentration.

One of the dangers of burnout is the pervasive ways it alters perspective. It is essential to take time off to discern the fact from the fiction when you think. In some cases, the pandemic is causing burning out, while for others they've discovered burnout it already had. Perhaps you've fallen off the job you were in months or decades ago, yet it was only after these severe situations for you to be able to feel the effects. The experts in health say that being burned out is a serious risk to the health of your body and mind in danger, and ignored, could cause greater negative consequences. The majority of those who suffer from this type of burning out say they did not do anything about the issue. Experts in the field of health agree that untreated stress could put your mental as well as physical health at risk The feelings and signs don't simply disappear on their own. It's particularly striking that the study found that 37% of people reported not doing anything to deal with the emotions.

There's good news that there are a lot of tried and tested strategies to deal the issue. If you're experiencing the signs of stress, it's crucial to take these concerns seriously and don't think it's a temporary issue and that they will pass disappear over time. Spend some time to reflect on your feelings, and a short distance away from work could help you identify the reasons for your emotions. If they are not atypical, and may be cured by taking better care of yourself. It is possible that you will start to get more sleep as well as more physical activity as well as feel the emergence of an optimistic outlook. The early signs could tempt you to proclaim a premature win. Early positive indicators are an indication that your plan works, but not proof of having completed the plan. The game of self-care can be long that requires you to keep going with it.

The effects of burnout are real at home working. It's not uncommon to seem like burning me out. When working from home, staying away from burnout and paying attention to our emotional and mental well-being is more essential than ever before. The process of reviving your burnt-out professional lifestyle is a constant process of pulling back, and undergoing a process that is self-examination. It's crucial to look closely of your day-to-day life and keep a journal in a way that records both your feelings as well as time usage. "By keeping a journal every day and looking back, you will be able to see and find patterns and triggers for the adjustments you have to implement. Make yourself accountable for your taking care of yourself. Establish a healthy, balanced lifestyle. It can be difficult to prioritise your needs and take care of yourself, but it is essential to be your highest performance to all you're doing. "When you're constantly stressed it is possible that your capacity to maintain an open mind is weakened. That is the time to talk with an outsider who is objective can be invaluable."

Preventive and Curative

Ways to Manage Burn Out

Micro-Breaks: When you get messy on the job making a mini-break to replenish your energy is an effective way to prevent burning out. Invigorating yourself through your day will keep you at a higher level of happiness and efficient condition. If you find yourself struggling to maintain focus, consider taking a brief break. Just a few minutes to clear your mind could assist in boosting your focus and efficiency. Micro-breaks can come in different forms and is essential to try out which type of break is the best. It might be a brief stroll, watching a short video footage or just a couple of minutes of quiet.

Prioritizing and distributing daily work load The importance of this is the long-term reduction of stress. Heavy workloads as well as potential burnout can be occasions to increase the empowerment of staff. Find out who is able to assume new roles and allow them to investigate. This is also an ideal time to rethink your ideas of what's possible.

You

It's more common than ever to delay your work It's true that procrastination is a threat to your mental wellbeing. If you're not setting objectives to work towards or even achieving that you feel you're not doing enough. Numerous studies suggest having goals you're actively striving to reach can improve the overall mood of your employees. A more positive outlook, naturally, reduces stress and makes your body in good shape, too. One of the main reasons is that we're all humans, and we mostly depend on other people for help.

Although you may contact your managers and colleagues via email, or schedule telephone or video conferences but not getting that instant face-to-face interaction could easily derail the spirit of your colleagues.

An overwhelming anxiety to be more: These fears of being required to perform more work because of someone else is probably unfounded and can cause a lot of stress on your health, and in turn, impact your work. In the end, wouldn't it be best to focus on doing the job you're supposed to do rather than add as much weight as is possible for the sake of being able to take on additional work?

You

Be sure to check your email every day: It's essential to create boundaries for yourself and to make an effort to avoid checking your email regularly. Make a schedule to check emails. Use a separate email ID used for office work.

Meetings are running over their designated time blocks. Set a every day's meetings at a certain time and alert other employees. Meet with the boss and discuss scheduling each day's meeting, unless very urgent.

You must stop "adulting" completely The consequences can be a significant impact on your mental health when you begin to become bored -- something that happens. It is a good idea to work out and then meditate for 30 mins each day before diving straight into your the work.

Trouble with relaxation: Having trouble resting in WFH could be an indication of burnout that has been overworked. For optimal performance at work it is essential to have regular times of rest to recharge your batteries. These periods of relaxation and relaxation help replenish your body and your mind. They are crucial in order to complete your work effectively.

Tiredness: If you're experiencing insomnia or constant exhaustion, speak with your doctor. Also, let the authorities know that you're suffering. If you're in need of help get the time away to get some sleep and to unwind.

Trouble Concentrating: It may be hard to increase the concentration of your employees and then get back to your routine. If you do take frequent breaks and are involved in projects that interest you, you will start to notice your focus and enthusiasm levels rise.

Staying out of social situations: Being connected with loved ones is an excellent method to relax and be satisfied when you're feeling down about your work. Be honest with the people closest to you. They could help you get perspectives on the problems you're facing and can encourage you to seek assistance if needed.

Being Unsatisfied: Talking to your friends, boss, and your family members about your concerns will help to eliminate these feelings.

Being a victim of a short fuse: Outbursts of emotion are an indication that it is time to have a rest and place the health of your family above everything other things. A break from your work for example, like a holidays, or taking the day to unwind in your home, can help ease your stress and put things in perspective. But if it does not help, consider consulting a doctor or therapist for a discussion of the thoughts and emotions. Remember that there's nothing wrong with seeking assistance, since there are more people who need to do this than you might think.

Physical ill-health: It's crucial to focus on your physical health before everything else. If you're experiencing stress at work, and this is getting worse for your overall health, make sure to allow time to take the time that you require to recuperate. Consult your physician for diagnoses and make sure your bosses are kept informed as to health issues. If you're looking for a job which will allow you to achieve a balanced work/life contact one of our professional recruiters today to aid you in finding the ideal job. Training could play a significant role in improving the health of your immunity system and also provide the energy needed for daily activities. Eating healthy and reducing alcohol and smoking will assist.

Workspace. Make a space for work, separate from the common areas of living as well as bedrooms. Set out your day's schedule - and think about the things you are able to accomplish. Take breaks and go for walk. Don't worry about household chores! You can put them off. Make sure you prioritize your work that is paid first.

Seek Support. Tell Your Boss You're Burned Out. Many companies provide counseling services for free via the Employee Assistance Programs (EAP). Inquire with your HR department to learn more about these programs. If they don't offer it any, you can find other sources for this. It is crucial to have support and the earlier it's received, the more effective. Engaging in open discussions about how you are negatively affected by stress can be an excellent way to create an environment of solidarity and love. Also, we must accept ourselves with kindness and set reasonable goals and learn assertive ways in communicating with our colleagues.

Mindfulness and meditation. Mindfulness improves self-awareness. This makes it simpler to control and manage feelings. Many times, we are stuck within a negative mental condition, and having a level of self-awareness can help us move from the negative mood towards a positive state. Being mindful. The practice of mindfulness helps us manage the emotions that in turn decreases anxiety, enhances mood, enhances sleep and boosts cognitive. Additionally, it reduces blood pressure and eases the pain of chronic illness.

Relaxing and recharging: Also, it is important to consider making sure you take time to spend time with and investing in your loved ones. Seek out silver lines. More time with your family members or sleep-ins more often and wearing Ugg boots throughout the day as well as extra coffee breaks. Remember that the scenario that we're in is evolving so that we can be able to enjoy a night out for dinner, and even make plans for holidays once again! As of now, even though we're all as a group, our responses will be different when we face our own particular issues. Don't be a skeptic about the challenges other people are facing.

How to Feel Better. Consider one of these:

Make sure you schedule the time with your friends that always bring a smile to your face. It means you'll need to reduce your work schedule. that are on your calendar. But it's what you're doing to be honest, isn't it?

Spend some time pampering yourself with some pampering. This could mean booking an appointment at the spa or tickets for a captivating performance you've read about It's time to rekindle your love of the lifestyle you've worked so hard to make to you.

Trim down your to-do list. If important things go unnoticed most likely, you've added more to your agenda than you can realistically manage.

Send work-related concerns to your supervisors. It might seem odd to highlight your frustration with those whom you think are at fault. However, if you view the conversation in the context of an intervention and not as a battle and you can be in a position to end those tensions for good.

Set up your objectives for the day for a renewed energy. A sense of burnout triggered by fatigue could indicate that you're more than fatigued, but are exhausted of the regular mundane routine.

Find methods to assume different responsibilities in similar fields to become more involved. You can join an organization connected to an area of your work you'd like additional experience.

Chapter 5: The Causes Of Boredom

The term "boredom" refers to a sense of indifference or a absence of enthusiasm or interest to one's activities or surroundings. It may be associated with emotions of frustration, restlessness or an disinterest. It is common to experience boredom and something all individuals experience at least once throughout their lives.

ADHD boredom, also known as boredom for those who suffer from attention deficit hyperactivity disorder (ADHD) can be caused by the difficulty of discovering activities that are interesting or exciting enough to keep their interest. The result could be feeling of agitation and constant desire to change things up or try new things. The people who suffer from ADHD might also have less tolerance to boring or repetitive activities that can lead to the feeling of boredom. It's important to remember that boredom is an everyday event and not exclusive for those who suffer from ADHD. It is, however, more prominent in people suffering from ADHD due to the particular problems they confront with managing their attention and concentration.

It is a frequent issue among people with ADHD (Attention deficit hyperactivity disorder). The cause can stem from various factors such as:

1. Repetitive or Unchallenging Tasks

This could be the reason of boredom for people with ADHD and for those who do not have ADHD. The feeling of boredom is common that may occur in those who are not involved in tasks which are challenging or stimulating enough to keep their interest. The people who suffer from ADHD might be more prone to feeling bored due to their propensity to be easily distracted and look for novelty and diversity of their surroundings.

In the case of people suffering from ADHD These kinds of jobs often require constant concentration, which is challenging to sustain. Furthermore, because these activities are not challenging, they could be viewed as boring which can lead to a absence of motivation and stimulation. The feeling of boredom is often frustrating and can cause a difficult time focusing on tasks makes it hard for people who suffer from ADHD to accomplish their goals or take part in activities which they consider boring.

To reduce boredom, people who suffer from ADHD could benefit from discovering methods to make their work more stimulating or challenging like through the addition of elements of fun or ingenuity to the work they do. It is also possible to benefit by looking for activities that match with their strengths and interests and strengths, which can assist to keep them interested and excited.

2. Limited Opportunities For Self-Expression

The people who suffer from Attention Deficit Hyperactivity Disorder (ADHD) frequently are unable to concentrate and become quickly bored. Lack of self-expression opportunities could be a significant contributing reason for the feeling of feeling of boredom. Self-expression is a vital way to express your creativity. It could help those with ADHD focus and remain active. If there aren't enough opportunities to express themselves individuals suffering from ADHD might be unable to locate activities that keep them engaged and entertained. This could lead to feeling of discontent, anxiety and a sense of feeling of boredom.

One of the best methods to ease boredom for people suffering from ADHD can be to provide the opportunity for self-expression. It could be as simple as painting, drawing, performing, singing as well as writing or participating in sports-related activities such as running. Additionally, it's essential to provide the opportunity for interaction with others to help in keeping people suffering from ADHD interested and entertained.

Additionally, having a structure as well as routine could be helpful. For those who suffer from ADHD typically require a clearly defined timetable and routine for staying active and focused. It could be as simple as setting a bedtime for the night and a specific area to complete homework and having set times to exercise as well as free time.

Being able to access a wide range of ways to express yourself can be a fantastic option to ease boredness in people suffering from ADHD. Additionally, it can provide the structure and routine that can keep them engaged and focused when they are engaged in their pursuits.

3. Social Isolation

Social isolation could be an important reason for boredom among people suffering from ADHD. ADHD or the attention deficit hyperactivity disorder is a neurodevelopmental condition characterized by a lack of concentration, impulsivity, as well as excessive activity.

This can cause it to be difficult for people who suffer from ADHD to take part in tasks which require constant attention, and develop and keep relationships with their peers. In the end, they might feel lonely from the rest of their friends and be bored as a result.

Social isolation is particularly difficult for people who suffer from ADHD as it may increase the severity associated with the condition. In particular, people who suffer from ADHD might have difficulties when it comes to social interaction and could find it difficult to engage in or keep conversations with friends. It can cause feelings of isolation and loneliness that can lead to boredom.

In addition, those who suffer from ADHD are likely to have difficulty coming up with activities that are enjoyable or stimulating enough that they retain their interest. It can lead to the feeling of being bored, and can result in a loss of motivation, and even low self-esteem.

It is essential for people who suffer from ADHD to have the opportunity to interact with other people and engage in activities that are worthwhile as well as enjoyable. It could mean looking for recreational or social events specially designed for people who suffer from ADHD as well as finding supportive family members or peers in helping provide an experience of belonging and feeling of belonging. Also, it can be helpful to seek out support from a professional in mental health for example, counselor or therapist, who can assist people with ADHD in identifying and addressing the root causes behind their loneliness and boredom.

4. Sensory Overload

Sensory overload could be an underlying cause of boredom among people suffering from ADHD in addition to for those who do not have ADHD. Sensory overload happens in people who are overloaded by all the information that is coming through their senses like the senses of sound, sight as well as smell, taste and. It can cause difficulty in paying attention, trouble in processing information and managing emotions, all of that can lead to a feeling of frustration.

If you have ADHD and sensory overload, it can be challenging due to the fact that they might already be struggling with controlling their emotions and attention. Additionally, they may feel more sensitive to certain stimuli and more likely to experience excessive sensory stimulation. It can cause feeling of agitation, anger or boredom, particularly during situations in which they are forced to concentrate on something for long periods of time for instance, in the classroom or at an extended gathering.

In order to manage the effects of the overload of sensory stimuli and to reduce the feeling of boredom, people who suffer from ADHD might benefit from methods that include having breaks, participating in exercise, playing with the fidget toy or other tools for sensory stimulation, as well as seeking ways to cut down on the amount of sensory stimuli they're exposed. It could also be beneficial working with a therapist or another professional in mental health to develop strategies to cope and discover methods to manage the effects of the overload of sensory stimuli.

5. Low Self-Esteem

Self-esteem issues can be an underlying cause of boredom among people suffering from ADHD because of a myriad of causes. For one, people with ADHD might have difficulties in executive functioning like making plans, organizing and finishing tasks. This could lead to low level of accomplishment and feelings of being unsatisfactory and can lead to feelings of self-worth and low self-esteem.

The second reason is that people with ADHD might have difficulty when it comes to social interactions, as well as forming and maintaining friendships. The result is feelings of loneliness and isolation that can lead to a low self-esteem.

Additionally, people suffering from ADHD are likely to have a hard time engaging and inspire their minds. This could lead to frustration and lack of enthusiasm, which may result in low self-esteem.

In the end, self-worth issues can create a vicious cycle for people with ADHD. A lack of motivation and boredom satisfaction that comes of ADHD may lead to a lower self-esteem. This could lead to boredom as well as a low motivation. It is crucial for people who suffer from ADHD to build confidence in themselves and find activities or activities that interest and motivate them to stop this vicious pattern.

6. Lack of Structure

People suffering from Attention-Deficit Hyperactivity Disorder (ADHD) frequently aren't organized and lack structures, and a lack of structure may cause the feeling of being bored. It is due to the fact that those suffering from ADHD typically require the clarity of a sense of direction and structure to remain motivated and involved when engaged in tasks. In the absence of structure, it could be difficult for people who suffer from ADHD to remain engaged and focused, which can lead to frustration.

In addition, those who suffer from ADHD are likely to have a strong desire for stimulation and novelty for staying interested. In the absence of organization, it may be difficult for them to locate tasks that are interesting as well as stimulating enough to keep their interest. The lack of structure can lead to feelings of boredom.

It's important to remember that, while the absence of organization can cause boredom in people with ADHD however it's not the sole reason. Others, like the absence of goals that are meaningful or lack of social relationships, may cause feeling bored in people who suffer from ADHD. It is essential for those suffering from ADHD to discover methods to establish the structure and motivation within their lives to keep them motivated and interested.

7. Inadequate Treatment

A lack of treatment for ADHD could cause boredness in those suffering from ADHD in several ways. For one, if people with ADHD don't receive the adequate treatment, they're likely to have difficulty focusing on their tasks or activities which aren't stimulating or stimulating.

If they are unable to pay and maintain attention, people are likely to become disinterested or even lose interest in the things. In addition, as people suffering from ADHD are often benefited by the structure, predictability as well as external assistance, insufficient care can result in being unable to organize, plan, and manage their own tasks. It can result in lack of ability to create or find worthwhile activities, and may cause boredom.

In addition, those suffering from ADHD might be bored due to lack of resources or assistance to participate in pursuits that are engaging and enjoyable. If they do not have the assistance or resources, people are likely to become bored rapidly or find it difficult to participate with activities relevant to their interests.

Chapter 6: Strategies For Managing Boredom In Individuals With Adhd

If you suffer from ADHD and are suffering from it, you might be having a difficult time coming up with ways to be engaging and stimulating enough to capture your attention. This can lead to feeling of agitation and the desire for continual excitement. In this post we'll look at strategies to manage ADHD boredom.

There is no way to entirely stay clear of any monotonous situation. However, you can develop strategies to you to make the situation more bearable. These tips are designed intended for those who have ADHD.

1. Channeling Bored Behaviors

There are many ways to play around with your hands that will keep you entertained and not get up. It could be the stress ball, drawing and making notes (try using an all-color pen) taping a pen onto your leg (so that it does not make a sounds) or playing around with a small rock. In case you're going to an uninteresting seminar or meeting, bring your tools for fidgeting with.

2. Preparing For The Unexpected

Make a boring pack. It's impossible to predict what you'll need to do if you wait at the doctor's appointment at a traffic stop, or standing in the line. To entertain yourself in those moments, pack bags with objects to keep you entertained like a collection of crosswords, Sudoku and a book to read, or apps installed on your phone or tablet you can use to pass the time when bored.

3. Making Time For Your Passions

You should spend time each day doing something you are passionate about. It may be more enjoyable to go through those boring times in your life when you know that in the future you will be able to engage in something fascinating.

4. Organizing Your Options

Write down a list of tasks that you enjoy. If you're bored, it is possible that you are unable to come up with an idea of something that you'd like to try. Make a list of your mobile and also at home. When you are bored, refer to your list and pick something to do.

5. Staying Curious About The World Around You

Discover something completely new. With tablets and phones at hand, it's simple to connect online and explore a topic. With your checklist of activities that are interesting, you should keep an agenda of subjects you'd like to study. Spend some time during a wait room, waiting for an airplane or on the line to launch your web browser to start discovering something new.

6. Building a Productive And Stimulating Schedule

Maintain your day organized and active. If you've already laid your activities during the day, you have the least chance that you'll be bored. Set out your schedule however don't forget some unplanned situations that arise in the spur of the moment.

7. Checking Off Daily Necessities

Prepare for the boring things you will do. Bring your fidget toys with you. You must ensure that you've had a meal or used the bathroom, and you're dressed in a comfortable way. Reduce distractions, so that you're less likely to be required to go out.

8. Exercise

Exercise has been shown to be beneficial for managing symptoms of attention-deficit/hyperactivity disorder (ADHD). It helps increase focus, concentration and impulse control in addition to reducing the amount of impulsivity and hyperactivity.

Physical exercise can help enhance sleep and sleep, which can be affected in those who suffer from ADHD. This can reduce anxiety and boost mood each of which is caused by people suffering from ADHD.

Alongside the direct impact in ADHD symptoms, exercising can be beneficial in indirect ways. Exercise can boost self-esteem and social abilities, as well as provide the feeling of satisfaction and achievement. This can be especially crucial for people suffering from ADHD and other disorders, who might struggle in social situations and suffer from an insecure self-esteem as a result of the problems.

9. Changing Your Perspective

Participate in what's taking place. If you're in the lecture that you think is boring look at the subject in a new way so that it is interesting. Notes. Ask questions. If you're actively engaged, the less likely you become bored.

10. Making Ordinary Moments Entertaining

You can play games with your brain. If you're in a queue, think of how many people spot wearing yellow shirts Look around, and make a list of. If you're stuck in traffic, take a look at license plates and see the number of states you will discover.

11. Becoming Your Own Expert

Find out the signs of boredom. Know the signs of. Watch out for signs that your brain is telling you that it's being bored. Do you get squirmy? Irritable? Angry? How do you handle boredom could help you to put strategies in place right away prior to your boredom getting your in problems.

12. Find a Mentor Or Support Group

A mentor or support group is an effective way of managing ADHD (attention to hyperactivity deficit). Mentors are able to provide assistance and guidance when you face the difficulties that come with ADHD. They can assist you to develop strategies to manage the symptoms you experience, provide emotional support, and provide encouragement in achieving your objectives.

Support groups can serve as a useful support for individuals suffering from ADHD. Through a support group it is possible to connect with other people who share similar challenges and experiences. The sharing of your successes and struggles in a group can make you feel less alone and more accepted. This can be also an opportunity to receive useful advice and suggestions on managing ADHD.

If you are looking for the right mentor or support group, begin by asking your doctor or mental health specialist to recommend a mentor or support group. It is also possible to inquire for local groups or support groups for individuals with ADHD and search the internet for forums or groups which could be beneficial. It could take a bit of time to identify the best tutor or group of support, but it's well worth the effort in terms of the assistance and advice that you get.

Chapter 7: The Role Of Medication

Treatment for Attention Deficit Hyperactivity Disorder (ADHD) generally is a mixture of medication as well as treatment. It is a great solution to lessen the signs of ADHD such as boredom through helping increase focus and concentration and regulating the impulsive behaviour as well as reducing excessive activity. Therapy however helps people with ADHD develop strategies for coping and techniques to control the symptoms they experience and improve their general functioning. When combined, therapy and medications are a viable therapy approach to reduce the boredom of people and improving the overall satisfaction for people who suffer from ADHD.

Medication for ADHD

Treatment with medication is usually the initial method of treating ADHD especially for those who suffer from persistent or extreme signs. There are many types of medication that are typically employed in treating ADHD which include stimulants, non-stimulants and antidepressants. These medications, which include Ritalin as well as Adderall are effective in increasing the amount of neurotransmitters that are found in the brain that can aid in improving concentration and focus, and also reduce the impulsive behaviors.

The non-stimulant medicines, such as Strattera and Intuniv which work similarly, but don't affect your central nervous system the same way in the same way as stimulants. Antidepressants like Wellbutrin as well as Prozac are also utilized in treating ADHD especially in those who suffer from comorbidities like anxiety or depression.

It can be helpful at reducing boredom among people who suffer from ADHD through enhancing the ability of them to focus and concentrate on things, which makes tasks more interesting and fun. The medication can also assist in manage impulsive behaviour, which makes it simpler for those who suffer from ADHD to regulate their impulses and take more deliberate decisions regarding how they spend their time.

But it's crucial to remember that treatment can't be the only solution for addressing all the signs of ADHD It is usually necessary to integrate the use of medication with other methods for treatment including therapy in order to get the most effective outcome.

Therapy for ADHD

Therapy is an essential part of the treatment process for those suffering from ADHD specifically by helping them develop techniques for coping and to deal with their issues and enhance their general functioning. The therapy can come in many kinds, like the individual, the family and groups therapy. Common approaches for treatment for ADHD comprise cognitive-behavioral therapies (CBT) that assists people to recognize and alter bad habits and thoughts which contribute to their symptoms and social skills education, that helps people develop the necessary skills to be able to communicate effectively with others. Also, parents' education, which assists parents be aware of and help their children's needs.

Therapy is particularly beneficial to reduce boredom among people who suffer from ADHD through providing the resources they require to control their problems and discover meaning and purpose within their life. In particular, it can aid individuals to recognize and overcome negative thoughts which cause boredom and training in social skills helps individuals develop the necessary skills to build meaningful relationships to others, and also find pleasure when engaging in the activities they enjoy. In addition, therapy may help those suffering from ADHD to recognize their strengths and passions as well as develop strategies for reaching their dreams and finding happiness throughout their day-to-day life.

Conclusion: Medication and therapy are two essential components in the treatment process for decreasing boredom for people suffering from ADHD. The use of medication can improve concentration and focus, as well as control impulsive behaviors, which makes people with ADHD to participate in their various activities and have fun in their life.

Therapy is able to provide patients with the skills that they require to control the symptoms they experience and gain the meaning and motivation throughout their day-to-day life. Therapy and medication is a successful therapy approach to reduce anxiety and increasing general quality of life for people suffering from ADHD.

The Impact Of Boredom On The Daily Lives Of Individuals With ADHD

It is possible that boredom will have an influence on those suffering from ADHD at any time, from adolescence as well as in adulthood. ADHD also known as ADHD, also known as attention deficit hyperactivity disorder is a neurodevelopmental condition characterized by a lack of sustained focus, impulsivity and high levels of activity. This can cause it to be hard for people suffering from ADHD to cope with boredom since they might be more sensitive to stimulation. They may also struggle to take part in activities which do not provide enough excitement or novelty.

As we grow older, boredom may result in a myriad of undesirable outcomes for those who suffer from ADHD which include:

1. Instability: When children who suffer from ADHD get bored, they might become bored and are less inclined to participate with the activities. It can result in lower performance and performance in schools and other formal settings.

2. Increased Impulsivity: Being bored could increase the chances teens with ADHD may engage in risky or risky behavior, since they might seek novelty or stimuli to relieve their bored. It can lead to more risk-taking, and even risky actions.

3. A rise in frustration: The feeling of boredom may cause frustration and anger among adolescents suffering from ADHD because they find it difficult to concentrate or participate in pursuits that don't draw their interest. It can cause problems when it comes to social interactions as well as relationships with adults and peers.

4. Reduced social interactions: A lack of interest may lead to social loneliness and decrease in social interactions, because teenagers suffering from ADHD might not be as motivated to take part in things

that aren't the interest of their. The result is the absence of opportunities for them to develop social skills and to make significant connections with other people.

Even in adulthood, boredom could remain a negative influence for people suffering from ADHD such as:

1. Reduced Productivity: A lack of interest can cause a loss of motivation as well as difficulty in concentrating and result in reduced productivity in the workplace or in other workplaces.

2. Increased Risk-Taking: The boredom of life can result in impulsive behaviours among people suffering from ADHD that can result in an increase risks and possibly dangerous behavior.

3. Reduced satisfaction: A lack of interest can result in a lack of satisfaction and

satisfaction everyday life. Those who suffer from ADHD might not be able to participate in pursuits which keep their attention.

4. Reduced Social Connection: Apathy could lead to loneliness and decrease in social interactions, which can lead to the absence of meaningful connections with other people.

Chapter 8: Supporting Individuals With Adhd

There are a variety of ways other individuals can assist those who suffer from Attention Deficit Hyperactivity Disorder (ADHD). Strategies that could assist are:

Provide understanding and patience People suffering from ADHD might have difficulty with activities that are simple for other people but may require additional time as well as support in completing the tasks. It's useful to provide empathy and compassion and not criticize or a sense of frustration.

1. Create order and routine A consistent routine and clearly defined expectations are beneficial for people suffering from ADHD. People can assist those who suffer from ADHD through helping establish and maintain a well-organized

setting, for example by setting up a calendar for tasks as well as activities. They can also use visual aids for staying well-organized.

2. Promote Self-Advocacy: People who suffer from ADHD could benefit from knowing how to advocate on their own behalf and articulate their requirements. Others can help those suffering from ADHD by informing them to speak out and request assistance or accommodations when they need it.

3. Help with emotional issues Help with Emotional Support ADHD can be difficult people with ADHD can benefit by having a support group of friends and family that can provide support and compassion.

4. Get educated on ADHD If you know about ADHD and its symptoms, the more prepared to assist those suffering from

this condition. You might want to consider reading about ADHD and speaking to healthcare specialists, and looking for information such as support groups and online communities.

It's crucial to recognize that every person with ADHD is individual, so the types and amounts of assistance they require may differ. It is possible working with a health specialist or another qualified expert to identify the best methods to support a person suffering from ADHD.

Strategies that people with ADHD can help their own needs.

It could be beneficial to those who suffer from ADHD to discover things to do and hobbies which are stimulating and engaging. Here are some ideas to find hobbies and activities which can be fun and useful:

1. Physical Activity: Physical exercises including dancing, sport or yoga can help those who suffer from ADHD since they provide an outlet for excessive energy as well as help to improve concentration and focus.

2. Creative Pursuits: Activities like music, art or writing are excellent ways for people suffering from ADHD to be creative and express their creativity.

3. Activities that demand concentration and focus: Games like puzzle solving crossword or puzzles that require concentration, as well as video games may help people suffering from ADHD increase their ability to concentrate and focus.

4. Social Events: Engaging in a variety of social activities like becoming a member of a club or volunteering could be an excellent opportunity for those who

suffer from ADHD to make connections with people and to feel a sense achievement and purpose.

It can also be beneficial to those suffering from ADHD to test a wide range of interests and sports in order to discover what's most beneficial for their needs. It's crucial to select things that are fun and enjoyable, since it can assist people with ADHD keep their interest and enthusiasm.

The Importance Of Addressing Boredom In Individuals With ADHD

Inability to address boredom among people suffering from attention deficit hyperactivity disorders (ADHD) could cause a range of adverse consequences. The effects of boredom include decreased motivation, a poor performance in school as well as behavioral issues, that may have an lasting effect on a person's well-being.

If boredom isn't addressed, people suffering from ADHD could have problems staying focused in class or at work. This could result in low academic performance or poor job productivity. It can also have an adverse influence on their overall achievement as well as their chances of advancement.

The boredom of a person can lead to behaviors that are problematic, for example being a bit impulsive or engaging in dangerous actions. It can cause negative outcomes for an individual and for the people who are around them.

If boredom is untreated, it may result in feelings of discontent as well as low self-esteem. an absence of sense of purpose. It can also have an adverse effect on a person's wellbeing and mental well-being.

However the treatment of boredom among people suffering from attention deficit hyperactivity disorders (ADHD) could bring about numerous positive effects. A few of the possible benefits to addressing boredom during ADHD instances include:

Better academic performance discovering ways to boost enthusiasm and involvement in the activities of those who suffer from ADHD might be more inclined to be attentive in the classroom and do better in academics.

www.ingramcontent.com/pod-product-compliance
Lightning Source LLC
Chambersburg PA
CBHW070734020526
44118CB00035B/1318